Daily Goals Journal
by b^{pro}ookmark™

Achieving your
goals through
daily action

Dr. Roger D. Smith

Daily Goals Journal by ProBookmark: Achieving your goals through daily action

© Copyright 2012 by Roger Smith. All rights reserved. No part of this book may be reproduced or transmitted in any form or by any means, electronic or mechanical, including photocopying, recording, or by any information storage and retrieval system, without written permission from the author. For information address Modelbenders Press, P.O. Box 781692, Orlando, Florida 32878.

Modelbenders Press books may be purchased for business and promotional use or for special sales. For information please contact the publisher.

PRINTED IN THE UNITED STATES OF AMERICA

Visit our web site at www.modelbenders.com

Designed by Adina Cucicov at Flamingo Designs
Cover image: © gunnar3000—Fotolia.com

The Library of Congress has cataloged the paperback edition as follows:

Smith, Roger
    Daily Goals Journal by ProBookmark: Achieving your goals through daily action.
    Roger Smith. – 1st ed.
    1. Personal Growth – Success   2. Business Motivational
    3. Christian Life – Spiritual Growth
    I. Roger Smith II. Title

ISBN 978-0-9843993-5-2

Daily Goals Journal by ProBookmark™

BENJAMIN FRANKLIN WAS ONE of the first self-made millionaires in the United States of America and one of the first to explore the methods for becoming a successful person. In his autobiography, Franklin describes the process of self-improvement that he used to achieve his goals over many years. He created a goal journal like this one. His "little book" listed "13 Habitudes" that he wanted to achieve in his life. Then he devoted one page to focusing on and improving each habit individually. Franklin understood that his plan for self improvement could not reside in the dark recesses of his mind. This important plan needed to be captured on paper, it needed to be in front of his eyes, and it needed to be in his thoughts every day. His original ideas on goal setting and action planning are what made him one of the most successful people in America and one of the most important founders of a new country.

This *Daily Goals Journal* is your tool for following in the footsteps of Benjamin Franklin and thousands of other successful people who have come after him.

We all have dreams of doing great things, leaving our mark, and making the world a better place because we lived in it. But most of us do not take any actions toward achieving those dreams.

Daily Goals Journal
by bookmark™

People do not have a plan for moving from where they are today to where they want to be tomorrow. As a result, tomorrow comes and they are in exactly the same place that they were in yesterday and the day before that, and all of the days that have passed through their fingers.

People who are growing, changing, achieving their goals, and making their dreams come true handle their days very differently. Like Franklin, they write their goals down in a place that will be with them all day. Like Franklin, they have a plan of action to work on those goals every day. Like Franklin, they accomplish their goals one day at a time. These are the people who make the biggest contributions in society, government, religion, business, neighborhoods, families, and their inner lives. These are the people that you want to imitate.

This *Daily Goals Journal* is the perfect place to capture your goals and to follow an action plan for achieving them. Turn to the first page and make a complete list of your goals. Then use the journal to pick one goal to focus on each day.

We all have habits that we follow every single day. These habits are built from years of repetition. Tracking your goals and taking daily actions on them needs to become one of these habits for you. Use this journal religiously and consistently every day for one month and it will become part of your daily routine. Carry it with you through the day and capture the progress you are making. Review your past successes and be encouraged that you are achieving your goals one day at a time.

How to use Daily Goals Journal by ProBookmark™

You can look at this goal journal and understand instantly what you are supposed to do with it. The format is self-explanatory. But here are some tips that will help you get the most out of this powerful tool.

Goal Summary

1. **Goal List.** Make a complete list of all of the goals you are trying to achieve. Do not be shy. Do not hold back. Capture them all. Some people have two goals and others have twenty. Be true to your inner voice and let all of them come out on the paper. Do not worry that there are too many or too few. Now that you are working on them every day, you will balance them to your right number over time.

2. **Target Date.** If you have a definite year, moth, or date when a goal must be accomplished, then write it down. Some goals are so big that they may take years to accomplish, some may take a lifetime. But there are also goals that can be achieved in one week, one month, or one semester.

3. **Category.** Tag your goals with a primary category. Everyone has a different focus of their life. So you may have more spiritual goals than financial goals. But you should have goals in

several different categories. Some of the most common goal categories are: Spiritual, Financial, Social, Business, Education, Family, and Health. And feel free to create your own custom categories.

Daily Plan

1. **Goal.** Write the goal at the top of the page and include the number from the Goal Summary page. This will help you keep track of those you have focused on and those that are not getting attention.

2. **Date.** Enter today's date and the goal target date, if there is one. This will reinforce the urgency of making progress on each goal to achieve it by the target date.

3. **Morning: Visualization.** Each morning take a few moments to close your eyes and visualize the goal. This visualization should be a bright picture with vibrant colors and dynamic action. This will only take one minute, but it is important to stamp the goal into your memory and your plan for the day. Write down the images that you see during this visualization.

4. **Afternoon: Action Plan.** Describe the actions that you are planning on taking to achieve this goal. What can you do today to move one step closer to your goal? Feel free to add to this list throughout the day. Action ideas will come to you at odd times. Capture them here.

5. **Afternoon: Action Results.** Later in the day describe the actions that you have taken and the results that you have achieved. Sometimes one of the results will be to identify new actions to be taken in the future.

6. **Afternoon: Inspiration.** How do you feel about the goal and your actions? Is the goal becoming more real? Are you getting closer to achieving it? Describe the feelings, the images, the sounds, the people, and the celebration of reaching your goal.

7. **Progress.** Rate today's progress between one and five stars.

50 Day Progress

1. **Goal List.** Summarize the progress you have made toward each goal. Rewrite a summary of the goal and whether you are closer to achieving it than you were when you started.

2. **Goal Progress.** As with your daily progress tracking on each goal, color in the number of stars that represent your cumulative progress toward achieving this goal. At the beginning most goals will have just one star. But over time many of them will move up to three, four, and five stars.

Daily Goals Journal
by bookmark™

Celebrate & Repeat

You will not reach all of your goals in the 100 days that can be recorded in one of these books. When you reach the end of the journal you should celebrate your determination, discipline, and progress. If you are the kind of person who can stick with the goal journal for 100 days, then you are the kind of person who can achieve all of their goals.

When you finish celebrating, get another *Daily Goal Journal* and keep marching forward.

You are on a path to becoming the person you dream of being. The *Daily Goals Journal* is just one tool to help you get there. Don't ever give up. Always believe that you can reach your dreams and accomplish your goals because you are the kind of person who works on them daily.

Best Wishes,
Roger Smith

Goal Summary

Daily Goals Journal
by bookmark™

target date

1 ....
....
2 ....
....
3 ....
....
4 ....
....
5 ....
....
6 ....
....
7 ....
....
8 ....
....
9 ....
....
10 ....
....
11 ....
....
12 ....
....

Goal Summary

Daily Goals Journal
by bookmark™

target date

13 ....

14 ....

15 ....

16 ....

17 ....

18 ....

19 ....

20 ....

21 ....

22 ....

23 ....

24 ....

Daily Goal Tracker

Daily Goals Journal
by bookmark™ pro

goal # ....
date .... target date ....

MORNING

visualization ....
....
....
....

action plan ....
....
....
....

AFTERNOON

action results ....
....
....
....

inspiration ....
....
....
....

write it again ....
....
....
....

progress ☆☆☆☆☆

Daily Goal Tracker

Daily Goals Journal
by bookmark™

goal # ....
date .... target date ....

MORNING

visualization ....
....
....

action plan ....
....
....
....

AFTERNOON

action results ....
....
....
....

inspiration ....
....
....

write it again ....
....
....

progress ☆☆☆☆☆

Daily Goal Tracker

Daily Goals Journal
by bookmark[pro]™

goal # ....
date .... target date ....

MORNING

visualization ....
....
....

action plan ....
....
....

AFTERNOON

action results ....
....
....

inspiration ....
....
....

write it again ....
....
....

progress ☆☆☆☆☆ 5

Daily Goal Tracker

Daily Goals Journal
by bookmark™

goal # ....

date .... target date ....

MORNING

visualization ....
....
....

action plan ....
....
....
....

AFTERNOON

action results ....
....
....

inspiration ....
....
....

write it again ....
....
....

progress ☆☆☆☆☆

Daily Goal Tracker

Daily Goals Journal
by bookmark™

goal # ....

date .... target date ....

MORNING

visualization ....
....
....

action plan ....
....
....

AFTERNOON

action results ....
....
....

inspiration ....
....
....

write it again ....
....
....

progress ☆☆☆☆☆   7

Daily Goal Tracker

Daily Goals Journal
by bookmark™

goal # ....
date .... target date ....

MORNING

visualization ....
....
....

action plan ....
....
....

AFTERNOON

action results ....
....
....

inspiration ....
....
....

write it again ....
....
....

progress ☆☆☆☆☆

Daily Goal Tracker

Daily Goals Journal
by bookmark™

goal # ....
date .... target date ....

MORNING

visualization ....
....
....

action plan ....
....
....

AFTERNOON

action results ....
....
....

inspiration ....
....
....

write it again ....
....
....

progress ☆☆☆☆☆   9

Daily Goal Tracker

Daily Goals Journal by bookmark™

goal # ....

date .... target date ....

MORNING

visualization ....
....
....

action plan ....
....
....

AFTERNOON

action results ....
....
....

inspiration ....
....
....

write it again ....
....
....

progress ☆☆☆☆☆

Daily Goal Tracker

Daily Goals Journal
by bookmark™

goal # ....
date ....   target date ....

MORNING

visualization ....
....
....
....

action plan ....
....
....
....

AFTERNOON

action results ....
....
....
....

inspiration ....
....
....
....

write it again ....
....
....
....

progress ☆☆☆☆☆

Daily Goal Tracker

Daily Goals Journal
by bookmark™

goal # ....

date .... target date ....

MORNING

visualization ....

....

....

action plan ....

....

....

AFTERNOON

action results ....

....

....

inspiration ....

....

....

write it again ....

....

....

progress ☆☆☆☆☆

Daily Goal Tracker

Daily Goals Journal
by bookmark™

goal # ....
date ....   target date ....

MORNING

visualization ....
....
....

action plan ....
....
....

AFTERNOON

action results ....
....
....

inspiration ....
....
....

write it again ....
....
....

progress ☆☆☆☆☆

Daily Goal Tracker

Daily Goals Journal
by bookmark™

goal # ....

date .... target date ....

MORNING

visualization ....
....
....

action plan ....
....
....

AFTERNOON

action results ....
....
....

inspiration ....
....
....

write it again ....
....
....

progress ☆☆☆☆☆

Daily Goal Tracker

Daily Goals Journal
by bookmark™

goal # ....

date .... target date ....

MORNING

visualization ....
....
....

action plan ....
....
....

AFTERNOON

action results ....
....
....

inspiration ....
....
....

write it again ....
....
....

progress ☆☆☆☆☆   15

Daily Goal Tracker

Daily Goals Journal
by bookmark™

goal # ....

date .... target date ....

MORNING

visualization ....
....
....

action plan ....
....
....

AFTERNOON

action results ....
....
....

inspiration ....
....
....

write it again ....
....
....

progress ☆☆☆☆☆

Daily Goal Tracker

Daily Goals Journal
by bookmark™

goal # ....
date .... target date ....

MORNING

visualization ....
....
....

action plan ....
....
....

AFTERNOON

action results ....
....
....

inspiration ....
....
....

write it again ....
....
....

progress ☆☆☆☆☆   17

Daily Goal Tracker

Daily Goals Journal
by bookmark™

goal # ....

date .... target date ....

MORNING

visualization ....
....
....
....

action plan ....
....
....
....

AFTERNOON

action results ....
....
....
....

inspiration ....
....
....
....

write it again ....
....
....
....

progress ☆☆☆☆☆

Daily Goal Tracker

Daily Goals Journal
by bookmark™

goal # ....

date .... target date ....

MORNING

visualization ....
....
....

action plan ....
....
....

AFTERNOON

action results ....
....
....

inspiration ....
....
....

write it again ....
....
....

progress ☆☆☆☆☆

Daily Goal Tracker

Daily Goals Journal
by bookmark™

goal # ....

date .... target date ....

MORNING

visualization ....
....
....

action plan ....
....
....

AFTERNOON

action results ....
....
....

inspiration ....
....
....

write it again ....
....
....

progress ☆☆☆☆☆

Daily Goal Tracker

Daily Goals Journal
by bookmark™

goal # ....

date .... target date ....

MORNING

visualization ....
....
....

action plan ....
....
....

AFTERNOON

action results ....
....
....

inspiration ....
....
....

write it again ....
....
....

progress ☆☆☆☆☆

Daily Goal Tracker

Daily Goals Journal
by bookmark[pro]™

goal # ....

date .... target date ....

MORNING

visualization ....
....
....

action plan ....
....
....

AFTERNOON

action results ....
....
....

inspiration ....
....
....

write it again ....
....
....

progress ☆☆☆☆☆

Daily Goal Tracker

Daily Goals Journal
by bookmark™ pro

goal # ....
date .... target date ....

MORNING

visualization ....
....
....
....

action plan ....
....
....
....

AFTERNOON

action results ....
....
....

inspiration ....
....
....

write it again ....
....
....

progress ☆☆☆☆☆

Daily Goal Tracker

Daily Goals Journal
by bookmark™

goal # ....

date .... target date ....

MORNING

visualization ....

....

....

action plan ....

....

....

AFTERNOON

action results ....

....

....

inspiration ....

....

....

write it again ....

....

....

progress ☆☆☆☆☆

Daily Goal Tracker

Daily Goals Journal
by bookmark™

goal # ....

date .... target date ....

MORNING

visualization ....
....
....

action plan ....
....
....

AFTERNOON

action results ....
....
....

inspiration ....
....
....

write it again ....
....
....

progress ☆☆☆☆☆

Daily Goal Tracker

Daily Goals Journal
by bookmark™

goal # ....

date .... target date ....

MORNING

visualization ....
....
....
....

action plan ....
....
....
....

AFTERNOON

action results ....
....
....
....

inspiration ....
....
....
....

write it again ....
....
....
....

progress ☆☆☆☆☆

Daily Goal Tracker

Daily Goals Journal
by bookmark™

goal # ....

date .... target date ....

MORNING

visualization ....
....
....

action plan ....
....
....
....

AFTERNOON

action results ....
....
....

inspiration ....
....
....

write it again ....
....
....

progress ☆☆☆☆☆

Daily Goal Tracker

Daily Goals Journal
by bookmark™

goal # ....

date .... target date ....

MORNING

visualization ....
....
....

action plan ....
....
....

AFTERNOON

action results ....
....
....

inspiration ....
....
....

write it again ....
....
....

progress ☆☆☆☆☆

Daily Goal Tracker

Daily Goals Journal
by bookmark™ [pro]

goal # ....
date .... target date ....

MORNING

visualization ....
....
....

action plan ....
....
....

AFTERNOON

action results ....
....
....

inspiration ....
....
....

write it again ....
....
....

progress ☆☆☆☆☆

Daily Goal Tracker

Daily Goals Journal
by bookmark™

goal # ....
date .... target date ....

MORNING

visualization ....
....
....

action plan ....
....
....

AFTERNOON

action results ....
....
....

inspiration ....
....
....

write it again ....
....
....

progress ☆☆☆☆☆

Daily Goal Tracker

Daily Goals Journal
by bookmark™

goal # ....
date .... target date ....

MORNING

visualization ....
....
....

action plan ....
....
....

AFTERNOON

action results ....
....
....

inspiration ....
....
....

write it again ....
....
....

progress ☆☆☆☆☆

Daily Goal Tracker

Daily Goals Journal
by bookmark™

goal # ....

date .... target date ....

MORNING

visualization ....
....
....
....

action plan ....
....
....
....

AFTERNOON

action results ....
....
....
....

inspiration ....
....
....
....

write it again ....
....
....

progress ☆☆☆☆☆

Daily Goal Tracker

Daily Goals Journal
by bookmark™

goal # ....
date .... target date ....

MORNING

visualization ....
....
....

action plan ....
....
....

AFTERNOON

action results ....
....
....

inspiration ....
....
....

write it again ....
....
....

progress ☆☆☆☆☆   33

Daily Goal Tracker

Daily Goals Journal
by bookmark™

goal # ....
date .... target date ....

MORNING

visualization ....
....
....

action plan ....
....
....
....

AFTERNOON

action results ....
....
....

inspiration ....
....
....

write it again ....
....
....

progress ☆☆☆☆☆

Daily Goal Tracker

Daily Goals Journal
by bookmark™

goal # ....

date .... target date ....

MORNING

visualization ....
....
....

action plan ....
....
....

AFTERNOON

action results ....
....
....

inspiration ....
....
....

write it again ....
....
....

progress ☆☆☆☆☆

Daily Goal Tracker

Daily Goals Journal
by bookmark™

goal # ....

date .... target date ....

MORNING

visualization ....
....
....

action plan ....
....
....

AFTERNOON

action results ....
....
....

inspiration ....
....
....

write it again ....
....
....

36   progress ☆☆☆☆☆

Daily Goal Tracker

Daily Goals Journal
by bookmark™

goal # ....

date .... target date ....

MORNING

visualization ....
....
....

action plan ....
....
....

AFTERNOON

action results ....
....
....

inspiration ....
....
....

write it again ....
....
....

progress ☆☆☆☆☆

Daily Goal Tracker

Daily Goals Journal
by bookmark™

goal # ....

date .... target date ....

MORNING

visualization ....
....
....

action plan ....
....
....

AFTERNOON

action results ....
....
....

inspiration ....
....
....

write it again ....
....
....

progress ☆☆☆☆☆

Daily Goal Tracker

Daily Goals Journal
by bookmark™

goal # ....

date ....   target date ....

MORNING

visualization ....
....
....

action plan ....
....
....

AFTERNOON

action results ....
....
....

inspiration ....
....
....

write it again ....
....
....

progress ☆☆☆☆☆

Daily Goal Tracker

Daily Goals Journal
by bookmark™

goal # ....

date .... target date ....

MORNING

🗨 visualization ....
....
....

❗ action plan ....
....
....

AFTERNOON

❗ action results ....
....
....

💡 inspiration ....
....
....

❝ write it again ....
....
....

40 progress ☆☆☆☆☆

Daily Goal Tracker

Daily Goals Journal
by bookmark™

goal # ....
date .... target date ....

MORNING

visualization ....
....
....

action plan ....
....
....

AFTERNOON

action results ....
....
....

inspiration ....
....
....

write it again ....
....
....

progress ☆☆☆☆☆

Daily Goal Tracker

Daily Goals Journal
by bookmark™

goal # ....
date .... target date ....

MORNING

visualization ....
....
....

action plan ....
....
....

AFTERNOON

action results ....
....
....

inspiration ....
....
....

write it again ....
....
....

progress ☆☆☆☆☆

Daily Goal Tracker

Daily Goals Journal
by bookmark™

goal # ....

date .... target date ....

MORNING

visualization ....
....
....

action plan ....
....
....

AFTERNOON

action results ....
....
....

inspiration ....
....
....

write it again ....
....
....

progress ☆☆☆☆☆

Daily Goal Tracker

Daily Goals Journal
by bookmark™

goal # ....

date .... target date ....

MORNING

visualization ....
....
....

action plan ....
....
....

AFTERNOON

action results ....
....
....

inspiration ....
....
....

write it again ....
....
....

progress ☆☆☆☆☆

Daily Goal Tracker

Daily Goals Journal
by bookmark™

goal # ....

date .... target date ....

MORNING

visualization ....
....
....

action plan ....
....
....

AFTERNOON

action results ....
....
....

inspiration ....
....
....

write it again ....
....
....

progress ☆☆☆☆☆   45

Daily Goal Tracker

Daily Goals Journal
by bookmark™

goal # ....
date .... target date ....

MORNING

🗨 visualization ....
....
....

❗ action plan ....
....
....

AFTERNOON

❗ action results ....
....
....

💡 inspiration ....
....
....

❞ write it again ....
....
....

progress ☆☆☆☆☆

Daily Goal Tracker

Daily Goals Journal
by bookmark[pro]™

goal # ....
date .... target date ....

MORNING

visualization ....
....
....

action plan ....
....
....
....

AFTERNOON

action results ....
....
....

inspiration ....
....
....

write it again ....
....
....

progress ☆☆☆☆☆

Daily Goal Tracker

Daily Goals Journal
by bookmark™

goal # ....
date .... target date ....

MORNING

visualization ....
....
....

action plan ....
....
....
....

AFTERNOON

action results ....
....
....

inspiration ....
....
....

write it again ....
....
....

progress ☆☆☆☆☆

Daily Goal Tracker

Daily Goals Journal
by bookmark™

goal # ....
date .... target date ....

MORNING

visualization ....
....
....

action plan ....
....
....

AFTERNOON

action results ....
....
....

inspiration ....
....
....

write it again ....
....
....

progress ☆☆☆☆☆

Daily Goal Tracker

Daily Goals Journal
by bookmark™

goal # ....

date .... target date ....

MORNING

visualization ....
....
....

action plan ....
....
....

AFTERNOON

action results ....
....
....

inspiration ....
....
....

write it again ....
....
....

progress ☆☆☆☆☆

Daily Goal Tracker

Daily Goals Journal
by bookmark™

goal # ....
date .... target date ....

MORNING

🗨 visualization ....
....
....

❗ action plan ....
....
....

AFTERNOON

❗ action results ....
....
....

💡 inspiration ....
....
....

❝ write it again ....
....
....

progress ☆☆☆☆☆

Daily Goal Tracker

Daily Goals Journal
by bookmark™

goal # ....
date .... target date ....

MORNING

visualization ....
....
....

action plan ....
....
....

AFTERNOON

action results ....
....
....

inspiration ....
....
....

write it again ....
....
....

progress ☆☆☆☆☆

50-day Progress

Daily Goals Journal
by bookmark™

1 .... ☆☆☆☆☆

2 .... ☆☆☆☆☆

3 .... ☆☆☆☆☆

4 .... ☆☆☆☆☆

5 .... ☆☆☆☆☆

6 .... ☆☆☆☆☆

7 .... ☆☆☆☆☆

8 .... ☆☆☆☆☆

9 .... ☆☆☆☆☆

10 .... ☆☆☆☆☆

11 .... ☆☆☆☆☆

12 .... ☆☆☆☆☆

50-day Progress

Daily Goals Journal
by bookmark™

13 .... ☆☆☆☆☆

14 .... ☆☆☆☆☆

15 .... ☆☆☆☆☆

16 .... ☆☆☆☆☆

17 .... ☆☆☆☆☆

18 .... ☆☆☆☆☆

19 .... ☆☆☆☆☆

20 .... ☆☆☆☆☆

21 .... ☆☆☆☆☆

22 .... ☆☆☆☆☆

23 .... ☆☆☆☆☆

24 .... ☆☆☆☆☆

Daily Goal Tracker

Daily Goals Journal
by bookmark™

goal # ....
date .... target date ....

MORNING

visualization ....
....
....

action plan ....
....
....

AFTERNOON

action results ....
....
....

inspiration ....
....
....

write it again ....
....
....

progress ☆☆☆☆☆

Daily Goal Tracker

Daily Goals Journal
by bookmark™

goal # ....

date .... target date ....

MORNING

visualization ....
....
....

action plan ....
....
....

AFTERNOON

action results ....
....
....

inspiration ....
....
....

write it again ....
....
....

progress ☆☆☆☆☆

Daily Goal Tracker

Daily Goals Journal
by bookmark™ pro

goal # ....

date .... target date ....

MORNING

visualization ....
....
....

action plan ....
....
....

AFTERNOON

action results ....
....
....

inspiration ....
....
....

write it again ....
....
....

progress ☆☆☆☆☆

Daily Goal Tracker

Daily Goals Journal
by bookmark™

goal # ....

date .... target date ....

MORNING

visualization ....
....
....
....

action plan ....
....
....
....

AFTERNOON

action results ....
....
....
....

inspiration ....
....
....
....

write it again ....
....
....

58   progress ☆☆☆☆☆

Daily Goal Tracker

Daily Goals Journal
by bookmark™

goal # ....
date .... target date ....

MORNING

visualization ....
....
....

action plan ....
....
....

AFTERNOON

action results ....
....
....

inspiration ....
....
....

write it again ....
....
....

progress ☆☆☆☆☆   59

Daily Goal Tracker

Daily Goals Journal
by bookmark™

goal # ....

date .... target date ....

MORNING

visualization ....
....
....

action plan ....
....
....

AFTERNOON

action results ....
....
....

inspiration ....
....
....

write it again ....
....
....

progress ☆☆☆☆☆

Daily Goal Tracker

Daily Goals Journal
by bookmark™

goal # ....

date .... target date ....

MORNING

visualization ....
....
....

action plan ....
....
....

AFTERNOON

action results ....
....
....

inspiration ....
....
....

write it again ....
....
....

progress ☆☆☆☆☆   61

Daily Goal Tracker

Daily Goals Journal
by bookmark™

goal # ....

date .... target date ....

MORNING

visualization ....
....
....

action plan ....
....

....
....

AFTERNOON

action results ....
....

....

inspiration ....
....

....

write it again ....
....

....

progress ☆☆☆☆☆

Daily Goal Tracker

Daily Goals Journal
by bookmark[pro]

goal # ....

date .... target date ....

MORNING

visualization ....
....
....

action plan ....
....
....

AFTERNOON

action results ....
....
....

inspiration ....
....
....

write it again ....
....
....

progress ☆☆☆☆☆

Daily Goal Tracker

Daily Goals Journal
by bookmark™

goal # ....

date .... target date ....

MORNING

visualization ....
....
....

action plan ....
....
....

AFTERNOON

action results ....
....
....

inspiration ....
....
....

write it again ....
....
....

progress ☆☆☆☆☆

Daily Goal Tracker

Daily Goals Journal
by bookmark™ pro

goal # ....
date .... target date ....

MORNING

visualization ....
....
....

action plan ....
....
....

AFTERNOON

action results ....
....
....

inspiration ....
....
....

write it again ....
....
....

progress ☆☆☆☆☆

Daily Goal Tracker

Daily Goals Journal
by bookmark™

goal # ....
date .... target date ....

MORNING

visualization ....
....
....

action plan ....
....
....

AFTERNOON

action results ....
....
....

inspiration ....
....
....

write it again ....
....
....

progress ☆☆☆☆☆

Daily Goal Tracker

Daily Goals Journal
by bookmark™

goal # ....
date .... target date ....

MORNING

visualization ....
....
....

action plan ....
....
....

AFTERNOON

action results ....
....
....

inspiration ....
....
....

write it again ....
....
....

progress ☆☆☆☆☆

Daily Goal Tracker

Daily Goals Journal
by bookmark™

goal # ....

date .... target date ....

MORNING

visualization ....
....
....
....

action plan ....
....
....
....

AFTERNOON

action results ....
....
....
....

inspiration ....
....
....
....

write it again ....
....
....
....

progress ☆☆☆☆☆

Daily Goal Tracker

Daily Goals Journal
by bookmark™

goal # ....
date .... target date ....

MORNING

visualization ....
....
....

action plan ....
....
....

AFTERNOON

action results ....
....
....

inspiration ....
....
....

write it again ....
....
....

progress ☆☆☆☆☆

Daily Goal Tracker

Daily Goals Journal
by bookmark™

goal # ....
date .... target date ....

MORNING

visualization ....
....
....

action plan ....
....
....

AFTERNOON

action results ....
....
....

inspiration ....
....
....

write it again ....
....
....

progress ☆☆☆☆☆

Daily Goal Tracker

Daily Goals Journal
by bookmark™ [pro]

goal # ....

date .... target date ....

MORNING

visualization ....

....

....

action plan ....

....

....

AFTERNOON

action results ....

....

....

inspiration ....

....

....

write it again ....

....

....

progress ☆☆☆☆☆

Daily Goal Tracker

Daily Goals Journal
by bookmark™

goal # ....

date .... target date ....

MORNING

🗨 visualization ....
....
....

❗ action plan ....
....
....

AFTERNOON

❗ action results ....
....
....

💡 inspiration ....
....
....

❞ write it again ....
....
....

progress ☆☆☆☆☆

Daily Goal Tracker

Daily Goals Journal
by bookmark™

goal # ....

date ....   target date ....

MORNING

visualization ....
....
....

action plan ....
....
....

AFTERNOON

action results ....
....
....

inspiration ....
....
....

write it again ....
....
....

progress ☆☆☆☆☆   73

Daily Goal Tracker

Daily Goals Journal
by bookmark™

goal # ....
date .... target date ....

MORNING

visualization ....
....
....

action plan ....
....
....

AFTERNOON

action results ....
....
....

inspiration ....
....
....

write it again ....
....
....

progress ☆☆☆☆☆

Daily Goal Tracker

Daily Goals Journal
by bookmark™

goal # ....

date .... target date ....

MORNING

visualization ....
....
....

action plan ....
....
....
....

AFTERNOON

action results ....
....
....

inspiration ....
....
....

write it again ....
....
....

progress ☆☆☆☆☆   75

Daily Goal Tracker

Daily Goals Journal
by bookmark™

goal # ....
date .... target date ....

MORNING

visualization ....
....
....

action plan ....
....
....
....

AFTERNOON

action results ....
....
....

inspiration ....
....
....

write it again ....
....
....

progress ☆☆☆☆☆

Daily Goal Tracker

Daily Goals Journal
by bookmark™

goal # ....

date .... target date ....

MORNING

visualization ....
....
....

action plan ....
....
....

AFTERNOON

action results ....
....
....

inspiration ....
....
....

write it again ....
....
....

progress ☆☆☆☆☆

Daily Goal Tracker

Daily Goals Journal
by bookmark™

goal # ....

date .... target date ....

MORNING

visualization ....
....
....

action plan ....
....
....

AFTERNOON

action results ....
....
....

inspiration ....
....
....

write it again ....
....
....

progress ☆☆☆☆☆

Daily Goal Tracker

Daily Goals Journal
by bookmark™

goal # ....

date ....   target date ....

MORNING

visualization ....
....
....

action plan ....
....
....

AFTERNOON

action results ....
....
....

inspiration ....
....
....

write it again ....
....
....

progress ☆☆☆☆☆

Daily Goal Tracker

Daily Goals Journal
by bookmark™

goal # ....
date .... target date ....

MORNING

visualization ....
....
....

action plan ....
....
....

AFTERNOON

action results ....
....
....

inspiration ....
....
....

write it again ....
....
....

progress ☆☆☆☆☆

Daily Goal Tracker

Daily Goals Journal
by bookmark™

goal # ....

date .... target date ....

MORNING

visualization ....
....
....

action plan ....
....
....

AFTERNOON

action results ....
....
....

inspiration ....
....
....

write it again ....
....
....

progress ☆☆☆☆☆

Daily Goal Tracker

Daily Goals Journal
by bookmark™

goal # ....

date .... target date ....

MORNING

visualization ....
....
....

action plan ....
....
....

AFTERNOON

action results ....
....
....

inspiration ....
....
....

write it again ....
....
....

progress ☆☆☆☆☆

Daily Goal Tracker

Daily Goals Journal
by bookmark™ [pro]

goal # ....
date .... target date ....

MORNING

visualization ....
....
....

action plan ....
....
....

AFTERNOON

action results ....
....
....

inspiration ....
....
....

write it again ....
....
....

progress ☆☆☆☆☆   83

Daily Goal Tracker

Daily Goals Journal
by bookmark™

goal # ....

date .... target date ....

MORNING

visualization ....
....
....

action plan ....
....
....

AFTERNOON

action results ....
....
....

inspiration ....
....
....

write it again ....
....
....

progress ☆☆☆☆☆

Daily Goal Tracker

Daily Goals Journal
by bookmark™

goal # ....

date .... target date ....

MORNING

visualization ....
....
....

action plan ....
....
....

AFTERNOON

action results ....
....
....

inspiration ....
....
....

write it again ....
....
....

progress ☆☆☆☆☆

Daily Goal Tracker

Daily Goals Journal
by bookmark™

goal # ....

date .... target date ....

MORNING

visualization ....

....

....

action plan ....

....

....

AFTERNOON

action results ....

....

....

inspiration ....

....

....

write it again ....

....

....

progress ☆☆☆☆☆

Daily Goal Tracker

Daily Goals Journal
by bookmark^pro ™

goal # ....
date .... target date ....

MORNING

visualization ....
....
....

action plan ....
....
....
....

AFTERNOON

action results ....
....
....

inspiration ....
....
....

write it again ....
....
....

progress ☆☆☆☆☆   87

Daily Goal Tracker

Daily Goals Journal
by bookmark™

goal # ....

date .... target date ....

MORNING

visualization ....
....
....

action plan ....
....
....

AFTERNOON

action results ....
....
....

inspiration ....
....
....

write it again ....
....
....

progress ☆☆☆☆☆

Daily Goal Tracker

Daily Goals Journal
by bookmark™

goal # ....
date .... target date ....

MORNING

visualization ....
....
....

action plan ....
....
....

AFTERNOON

action results ....
....
....

inspiration ....
....
....

write it again ....
....
....

progress ☆☆☆☆☆

Daily Goal Tracker

Daily Goals Journal
by bookmark™

goal # ....

date .... target date ....

MORNING

visualization ....

....

action plan ....

....

AFTERNOON

action results ....

....

inspiration ....

....

write it again ....

....

progress ☆☆☆☆☆

Daily Goal Tracker

Daily Goals Journal
by bookmark™

goal # ....

date .... target date ....

MORNING

visualization ....
....
....

action plan ....
....
....

AFTERNOON

action results ....
....
....

inspiration ....
....
....

write it again ....
....
....

progress ☆☆☆☆☆

Daily Goal Tracker

Daily Goals Journal
by bookmark™

goal # ....
date ....   target date........................

MORNING

visualization ....
....
....

action plan ....
....
....
....

AFTERNOON

action results ....
....
....

inspiration ....
....
....

write it again ....
....
....

progress ☆☆☆☆☆

Daily Goal Tracker

Daily Goals Journal
by bookmark™

goal # ....

date .... target date ....

MORNING

visualization ....
....
....

action plan ....
....
....

AFTERNOON

action results ....
....
....

inspiration ....
....
....

write it again ....
....
....

progress ☆☆☆☆☆

Daily Goal Tracker

Daily Goals Journal
by bookmark™

goal # ....

date .... target date ....

MORNING

visualization ....
....
....

action plan ....
....
....

AFTERNOON

action results ....
....
....

inspiration ....
....
....

write it again ....
....
....

progress ☆☆☆☆☆

Daily Goal Tracker

Daily Goals Journal
by bookmark™

goal # ....
date .... target date ....

MORNING

visualization ....
....
....

action plan ....
....
....

AFTERNOON

action results ....
....
....

inspiration ....
....
....

write it again ....
....
....

progress ☆☆☆☆☆

Daily Goal Tracker

Daily Goals Journal
by bookmark™

goal # ....

date .... target date ....

MORNING

💭 visualization ....

....

....

⚡ action plan ....

....

....

AFTERNOON

⚡ action results ....

....

....

💡 inspiration ....

....

....

💬 write it again ....

....

....

progress ☆☆☆☆☆

Daily Goal Tracker

Daily Goals Journal
by bookmark™

goal # ....

date .... target date ....

MORNING

visualization ....
....
....
....

action plan ....
....
....
....

AFTERNOON

action results ....
....
....
....

inspiration ....
....
....
....

write it again ....
....
....

progress ☆☆☆☆☆   97

Daily Goal Tracker

Daily Goals Journal
by bookmark™

goal # ....

date .... target date ....

MORNING

visualization ....
....
....

action plan ....
....
....
....

AFTERNOON

action results ....
....
....

inspiration ....
....
....

write it again ....
....
....

progress ☆☆☆☆☆

Daily Goal Tracker

Daily Goals Journal
by bookmark™ (pro)

goal # ....
date .... target date ....

MORNING

visualization ....
....
....

action plan ....
....
....

AFTERNOON

action results ....
....
....

inspiration ....
....
....

write it again ....
....
....

progress ☆☆☆☆☆   99

Daily Goal Tracker

Daily Goals Journal
by bookmark™

goal # ....

date .... target date ....

MORNING

visualization ....
....
....
....

action plan ....
....
....
....

AFTERNOON

action results ....
....
....
....

inspiration ....
....
....
....

write it again ....
....
....

100

progress ☆☆☆☆☆

Daily Goal Tracker

Daily Goals Journal
by bookmark™

goal # ....
date .... target date ....

MORNING

visualization ....
....
....

action plan ....
....
....

AFTERNOON

action results ....
....
....

inspiration ....
....
....

write it again ....
....
....

progress ☆☆☆☆☆

Daily Goal Tracker

Daily Goals Journal
by bookmark™

goal # ....

date .... target date ....

MORNING

visualization ....
....
....

action plan ....
....
....

AFTERNOON

action results ....
....
....

inspiration ....
....
....

write it again ....
....
....

progress ☆☆☆☆☆

Daily Goal Tracker

Daily Goals Journal
by bookmark™

goal # ....
date .... target date ....

MORNING

visualization ....
....
....

action plan ....
....
....
....

AFTERNOON

action results ....
....
....

inspiration ....
....
....

write it again ....
....
....

progress ☆☆☆☆☆

Daily Goal Tracker

Daily Goals Journal
by bookmark™

goal # ....

date .... target date ....

MORNING

visualization ....
....
....

action plan ....
....
....

AFTERNOON

action results ....
....
....

inspiration ....
....
....

write it again ....
....
....

progress ☆☆☆☆☆

50-day Progress

Daily Goals Journal
by bookmark™

1 .... ☆☆☆☆☆

2 .... ☆☆☆☆☆

3 .... ☆☆☆☆☆

4 .... ☆☆☆☆☆

5 .... ☆☆☆☆☆

6 .... ☆☆☆☆☆

7 .... ☆☆☆☆☆

8 .... ☆☆☆☆☆

9 .... ☆☆☆☆☆

10 .... ☆☆☆☆☆

11 .... ☆☆☆☆☆

12 .... ☆☆☆☆☆

50-day Progress

Daily Goals Journal
by bookmark™

13 .... ☆☆☆☆☆

14 .... ☆☆☆☆☆

15 .... ☆☆☆☆☆

16 .... ☆☆☆☆☆

17 .... ☆☆☆☆☆

18 .... ☆☆☆☆☆

19 .... ☆☆☆☆☆

20 .... ☆☆☆☆☆

21 .... ☆☆☆☆☆

22 .... ☆☆☆☆☆

23 .... ☆☆☆☆☆

24 .... ☆☆☆☆☆

www.ingramcontent.com/pod-product-compliance
Lightning Source LLC
Chambersburg PA
CBHW031256290426
44109CB00012B/610